COLL] POEMS OF JOYCE NEILL

1960's – 2002

'And now in age I bud again'
George Herbert

Bright Pen

Visit us online at <u>www.authorsonline.co.uk</u>

A Bright Pen Book

Copyright © Joyce Neill 2007

ISBN 0-7552-1064-6
ISBN13: 978-0-755210-64-0

Authors OnLine Ltd
19 The Cinques
Gamlingay, Sandy
Bedfordshire SG19 3NU
England

This book is also available in e-book format, details of which are available at www.authorsonline.co.uk

FOREWORD

My mother started writing poetry again, after the early bursts which many write in their youth, in the late 1960's, as we her children were growing up. She ceased when her blindness made it impossible for her to write, and therefore to revise her work, and her very last poems date from 2002. Thus they cover that period of a woman's life rarely examined in literature yet so significant in the proportional length of a life.

There are three sections to the *Collected Poems*, which are primarily chronological in their ordering. *Children Grown* covers approximately twenty years. In these poems I feel the reflections on close family relationships reverberating and contrasting with a sombre theme of interaction and reaction to the Troubles.

In The Museum contains poems which are sadder and more bitter: she's older, the Troubles are intractable, and close relationships are no longer an unalloyed source of joy.

In *Last Poems* there is some resolution, through a kind of removal to a high plateau, where Time swirls and decelerates beneath her.

What I feel my mother has successfully done is to explore those emotional and spiritual landmarks of the later life, with vision and honesty.

Additionally, the undercurrent of a life perceived, at least as a poet, as one of exile adds poignancy to many of the poems.

For me the most significant poems are those in which, as Yeats wrote in ***Among School Children***

' my heart is driven wild:
She stands before me as a living child'.

Her skill and strength to me is that through her poetry she can reach back to all phases of her life from childhood to old age. In her 92nd year the lilac and lily-of-the-valley smell as strongly as they did when she first took them to school, aged nine.

Meg Beckett
February 2007

CONTENTS

CHILDREN GROWN

This section takes its title from the first poem, which is also the earliest here. I started writing verse again, on and off, in the 1960's when my children were growing up and I, in my forties, became involved again in medicine and experienced a sort of second adolescence. The first half-dozen poems here stem from this period. But the bulk of the poems are much later, post-retirement. They range from 1970, (*For William, Newly Born*), to 1990 when we left our rented flat, occupied after a bomb had wrecked our home, *(Transit Camp)*. During this period I had another renaissance, stimulated by my two spells at Woodbrooke, the Quaker College in Birmingham, and by attending Edith Devlin's Literature classes in The Department of Continuing Education at the Queen's University of Belfast. Some of these verses owe their existence directly to Edith.

It was as if creating a family and working in an interesting job had been sufficiently fulfilling, but when these interests ceased some sort of creative urge was released for verse.

Joyce Neill
1990

1. CHILDREN GROWN

CHILDREN GROWN

When you were very small, and wept
For sorrow or for pain,
You climbed upon my knee and crept
Within my arms, and comfort poured
Into your hearts like rain.

But now that you are grown, my dears,
And sorrows come again,
I can no longer stay your tears –
The ghostly umbilical cord
Tugs at my heart in vain.

MAGPIES

Walking in the park in pale winter sunshine,
Footsteps ringing on the frost-hard ground,
A magpie, elegant in black and white plumage
Landed and hopped around.
One for sorrow-
Sorrow for children grown and fled,
Sorrow for an old man long since dead,
Sorrow for ourselves long ago in our prime
Growing old now and stiff with the passing of time –
One for sorrow

Walking in the park in warm spring sunshine,
Birds singing madly and trees newly green,
Two magpies came flying, landed on the pathway
Proud to be seen.
Two for joy –
Joy for the childhoods shared by us all,
For much received and much to recall,
Joy in remembering the busy years
Filled with much laughter as well as some tears –
Two for joy.

One for sorrow
Two for joy
Three little girls and one little boy
And an old man, glimpsed among the trees -
They are here always, and always, with these,
Will be sorrow and joy.

ST. STEPHEN'S GREEN

Warmth of sunshine on last late flowers
Fluttering their flags in the stirring air,
Trees that tossed off their burden of leaves
To stand revealed as when spring was there.

And we, for that moment we shed the years,
Tossed off the burdens that time had brought,
Slipped back to our spring, to our Tir-na-nog,
When so little was lost and so much was sought.

FALL

Dead leaves in a London square
Fill my heart with memories,
Drifting through the fog-touched air,
Lifting on the autumn breeze.
Long ago, through such as these
We have often idled where
Dead leaves in a London square
Now fill my heart with memories.
Younger, greener, then we were
With hopes as high as these tall trees.
Now old dreams flutter, ill at ease,
Like dead leaves in a London square.

CARLINGFORD

Across the narrowing lough the Norman keep
Turns sightless eyes on palace of railway kings;
To the empty wharf that rots at the sea's assault
And the empty station where echoing footstep rings.

When alien knights kept watch from that grey tower
How long did they think their Norman rule would
last?
And when trains and ships were busy across the lough
Did travellers know their bustle would soon be past?

Lapped as we are in the present's tight cocoon,
We cannot see through the mushroom-clouded night
What lies ahead, what manner of life will remain,
When our own familiar world is lost to sight.

Only the massive Mournes behind the keep
And Carlingford mountain brooding over the way
Will still be links between Norman and railway king
And some future's children on Cranfield beach at
play.

CONNEMARA

This barren, beautiful country, where the wind
Howls over the brown bog, torturing the stunted trees;
Where huge waves, curling, crash on an empty strand
And adamant rocks pierce through the turbulent seas;
And by inland lakes, waves lapping at the edge
Eavesdrop on the incessant whispering of sedge;

Where, even when the storm ceases, and reluctant sun
Breaks through the mist and colour floods back again:
Purple of heath and loosestrife, gold of the whin
And blue sky mirrored in pools left by the rain –
This country excludes me; I cannot touch its soul.
I am the leper, watching from outside, by the hole.

DÉRACINÉE I (1962)

No longer part of this metropolitan arrogance,
Not yet absorbed into provincial pride,
Hovering in some rootless, unattached limbo
I am now outside.

The light brown, civilised Kent country,
The empty, expectant hop-poles in orderly line,
Even the reticent squares and the cockney voices
Are no longer mine.

And solitude, always before hoarded and precious,
Time has debased and made lonely, bitter and cold.
My heart is a hostage now, to reclaim lest I perish
Here, where I'm old.

DÉRACINÉE II (1990)

What will become of us who are transplanted,
Our roots dug up, placed in a soil untilled
By us? Time makes familiar the changes:
The oblique approach, the promise unfulfilled,
The words we know, but not their meaning here
Spoken as poetry from the people's lips,
The myths and legends glimpsed through twilit mist
And, most of all, light, and the landscape grips
Our hearts. We have been lulled to feel
Our new roots strong, sustaining, well-grown, real.

But twenty years of violence and discord,
Of hundreds dead, each one a nucleus
Of sorrow;
Rigidity of thought, and prejudices
Unaltered through the years;
The Celtic richness claimed by some – rejected
By others; all this brings doubts.
We are again uprooted: our new roots
Poisoned by old contamination of the soil.
We are outsiders still.

A BIRTHDAY GREETING

Many happy returns!
Return of what?
Of the Day
We used to say.
But may-
Be its true
Of you
Too?
You may return much further along The Way.
Well, I like to play
With words-
So anyway-
Many Happy Returns!

FOR WILLIAM, NEWLY BORN

Small, wrinkled, frail and infinitely wise,
Staring unfocussed with your violet eyes,
What distant unknown visions do you see?
Dear precious scrap of immortality.

GRANDCHILDREN

Grandchildren are our second chance
To know and love as if by right
Small bearers of immortality
Who can be lent us for a night.
To give and to receive embraces
From small hands touching faces-
It is most sweet.
Then too when they will greet
These parents-for-a-while
With welcoming smile,
We would do anything for them – and do
The whole day through.
And oh!
When they go
We miss them so!
Although we know
We are bit-actors only in their show,
Waiting in the wings to come and go.
But there we also can be blessed -
Taking a well-earned and much needed rest.

THREE POEMS ABOUT QUAKER MEETING FOR WORSHIP

I QUIET ROOM

Here, in this room, is the beginning.
Here, in each heart, lies the seed.
The growing Light, burning within the silence,
Illuminates our varying need.

Invisible, the movement of the Spirit,
Noiseless, the articulation of the Word.
Timeless, the gathered moments of the Meeting
In which we have both seen and heard.

We bring with us our private burdens,
The known and unknown needs of kin and friend,
And the world's pain and sorrow and injustice;
All can be shared, in this room, in the end.

II RATHFARNHAM

On to the gathered stillness of the Meeting
The children alight like feathers on a lake,
Or like birds, folding their wings and settling
On a smooth surface the ripples hardly break.

Their presence, scarcely apparent in muted
movements,
Small shufflings and little whispered questionings,
Is like the first faint-felt stretching of foetal limbs,
Or first heart-stirrings the Holy Spirit brings.

III   LAUNDRY

I lug this great laundry basket to Meeting,
Filled with damp, twisted bundles of problems, tasks
and commitments,
And I shake them out, one by one, and peg them on
the invisible line.
Then the Light shines on them and the Spirit blows
through them
And at the hour's end I take them down.
Most of them are smooth and aired and ready to put on
again;
A few are still a bit creased, but I can iron these later
At home.

TULIP MINISTRY

Tulips?
We all know what they are;
They grow up straight and tall
Outside a city hall,
Scarlet and pink and gold
They do as they are told,
Standing from dawn till dark
Bedded in public park,
Their goblet flowers, like hands in prayer,
Covering what is hid there.
And thus they do their duty
So all seems neat and pretty
In our fine city.

But not this tulip!

This tulip grew in a small pot
And all the stereotypes we know
This plant knew not.
And so
It grew so tall it bent
Its stem till the flower leant
Towards us. In the warm room
It opened wide in fullest bloom,
Its petals turning back so far
It now looked like a star
Or like a saucer upside down,
And all its secret mysteries were shown.

Remember – some miraculous-seeming flower
May be a tulip that has gone too far.

DYING AND DYEING

From profound silence, deep immersed, we rise
Still coloured from experiencing the vat;
But colour fades in common air so that
Only a faint hue lingers from the dyes.
Each time returning, something will remain,
Like cloth that's dipped and dipped again and dried,
Till colour, like the Spirit will reside,
And cloth and person show a lasting gain.

Dyeing and dying: both involve a change –
John Woolman died surrendering his will,
And Nicodemus puzzled at re-birth.

If we would turn around we must arrange
An alteration in our lives until
The Kingdom shows more clearly on the earth.

ULSTER FUNERAL

Four tall grandsons to carry her coffin,
Sons, nephews, cousins to follow in her wake.
Nothing left undone, all in right ordering,
She leaves for the churchyard and the final break.

Granddaughters, daughters, nieces, women cousins
Repair to the kitchen and spread out the tea.
Only one rebel granddaughter slips away to mourn her
There at the graveside where only men should be.

Dying at a great age, comforted and cared for,
Her long life acknowledged with gratitude and joy.
We meet now at table with talk of the family –
For word of this one's daughter, for news of that one's
boy.

KEEP SAYING NO

Children, when first they start to talk,
Learn to say 'No' long before 'Yes'.
It's safer to refuse to act
For fear of getting in a mess;
Better to keep the status quo
By sticking firmly to your NO.

In Irish there's no Yes or No
Whereas in English both are known;
Between two worlds, the Ulster Prods
Affirmatives have not yet shown;
But have they mastered the word NO?
Oh Yes! It's used like Billy-o!

THE KITCHEN SINK

Without the time spent at the kitchen sink
How would we think?
The dishes and the pans, the long hours spent,
Our poor backs bent –
The endless trail of vegetables, pared
We all have shared.
And we have known there's little need for thought
In tasks of this sort.
But this dull work can still release the mind
And it can find
Theories and fantasies and problems solved.
So – I'm resolved
That all who feature in our public places,
The well-known faces,
The politicians, and the violent men
Of gun or pen
Should spend some mandatory time and THINK
At the kitchen sink.
And there among the pots and pans and spuds
And warm soap suds,
Discover how to plan and to AGREE
And set us free.
Free from the hatreds, sorrows and the fears
Felt through the years.
For all need time spent at the kitchen sink
That they may THINK.

WANTED

Naked and vulnerable we all begin,
Naked and vulnerable we all remain
Beneath the varied garments we acquire
Stitched with experiences of joy and pain.

The lucky ones are lapped in love and care
Warmed with encouragement, dressed in esteem,
Coated in confidence, sure that their lives
Are based on reality and not a dream.

But the less fortunate wear a different garb.
Belittled, non-achieving, unfulfilled,
They clothe themselves in violence and resentment –
Thin, useless coverings that leave them chilled.
And then a voice cries loud
From the anonymous crowd;
'Send them to prison!'

GLENVEIGH CASTLE

I saw his photograph on the wall,
A blown-up picture (one wonders how he escaped the
same fate?)
He wears a romantic hat, and his hard, expressionless
eyes
Stare back at us.
Not a wicked face, but totally devoid of feeling.
How else could he have done it?
How could he make four hundred and fifty-four souls
Homeless, on a cold April morning?
Where did they go?
How many survived?
And what of the children?

Their children told their children and fed the long hard
memories.
They shake the transatlantic collecting boxes,
They watch the stoned police and the plastic bullets
With the same hard, expressionless eyes.

BELFAST – GOOD FRIDAY 1988

First the hope, an echo from Palm Sunday,
Gathered in warm sunshine under clear skies;
But the walk was muted, no crowds with glad cries
Ran out to meet us. What was there left to say?
Climbing the hill towards the open ground
Hope faded with the sunshine, skies turned dark.
The cross was raised, rain lashed us in the park,
Our prayers and readings made but a faint sound.

But then – the miracle – we turned around:
The clouds broke and the sun returned.
Over the stricken city and its strife
The perfect bow appeared, and so we found
The covenant renewed, as Noah learned,
God with mankind and all created life.

LILIES-OF-THE-VALLEY

I picked a bunch today.
I put them in a jug on the table,
I closed my eyes and buried my nose in their midst
And at once –
Short-circuiting the newer sense of sight
The old olfactory currents deeper than consciousness
Swept me back forty years.
Back to the small, fenced suburban garden
Which seemed world-sized to a child
And in May achieved its flowering summit of the
year:
The apple tree flushed against blue sky,
The generous spreading lilac perfuming the air,
And lilies-of-the-valley.
Only in May the surplus flowers spilled over
So I gathered bunches to take to school;
Armfuls of lilac for the windowsills, but for the desk,
Lilies-of-the-valley.
Through my closed eyes I see myself:
A plump brown child in brown-and-white striped
frock,
Brown blazer and panama hat and hat-band.
I walk up the Camden Road in the early sunshine
With a bouquet of lilac and a nosegay
Of lilies-of-the-valley.

GHOSTS

I have been wandering within the past,
Peering through dawn mists covering a land
Peopled by ghosts. Ghosts of the dead are here,
But of the living too; a motley band
Amongst whom I, a shade in many forms
From many stages of lives shared in part,
Move and converse and listen, and remember
How it was then – and still is in my heart.

First in the crowd, and only dimly seen,
Ghosts of my parents, long ago in Wales;
Younger than ever known by me, but still
Recognised from the many childhood tales
Told to me and my sister. She is with me too,
At many ages and in many places
From childhood to her death. And I have met
Friends from shared times, with loved familiar faces.

Strangest of all I meet my children and
I meet their children too. And I recall
Those warm, small forms cradled within my arms,
Now wandering here. Can they have grown so tall
In present times? Are they indeed the same?
What unique essence stays at the heart of these,
My loved companions through the changing years,
And lives in ghosts that now disturb my ease?

FOR EDITH DEVLIN

I   VIGNETTE

Embowered in magnolia,
Framed in forsythian gold,
Bathed in the benison of sunlight
After winter's cold.
Two students and their mentor,
Three heads bowed over the page,
Listening to words and verses
Of a former age.

II

Some have breathed new life into old books
And some have shared their fresh insight;
And some have led our steps abroad
To pastures new and landscapes bright.
And many a hostess greets her guests,
Shows them new friends and where to sit,
But only EDITH does all these
With grace, with scholarship and wit.
Now we rejoice that all may see
That EDITH is an MBE.

FOR GEORGE HERBERT
(in case souls migrate)

Dear gentle George, who often wrote
Of plants and flowers, and knew them well,
Which would your soul inhabit, if
It changed its home as some faiths tell?

Would it dwell in that brave-hued rose,
Still conscious of mortality?
And would it bud in age and show
Us glimpses of eternity?

Or would it take more modest form?
An evening primrose in the dark,
Scenting the air and bravely sharing
Its small share of the divine spark.

FOR URSULA
20.5.13 – 2.5.86

May will be your month always, now;
Birth and death both in this tender time of year.
Born into the scent of lilac and lily-of-the-valley,
To the sound of blackbird and thrush, early and
late,
And dying amid the myriad manifestations of new
green
Misting over bare trees.
Birth and death are both laboured, a struggle to
begin and end:
Green shoots push hard to break into the light,
And wind blows strongly to send petals whirling
to the ground.
But Light and Spirit are neither born nor die –
They still empower in other souls and places
And enfold new growth each May.

NAMING

When Adam named each living thing,
(Bidden in Eden by the Lord)
Each beast and fish, insect on wing,
Each plant and worm, each bird that soared,
He gained dominion over all:
Naming had put each one in thrall.
Knowledge of words and of a name
Gives power to those who use the same,
But as we age the words disperse,
Names we know well cannot be found,
Buried in memory underground.
There is a lesson in this verse:
When names escape, our powers go too –
A warning sign for me and you.

NOSTALGIA

When dusk deepens in the gloom
Of a December afternoon,
Dull, tawdry lights grow clear and true
And the old magic flows anew:
Tinsel turns silver, gilt to gold,
The tree's wide branches seem to hold
Rubies and emeralds. Now we hear
The beat of wings that fill the air –
Starlings (or angels?) seek the square.
Down dark side streets, diamonded pane
And jewelled windows shine again.

GIANT'S RING

A strange and haunted site – nobody knows
For certain, of its use.
Perhaps a place of ritual and assembly?
In mellow autumn sunshine and cool breezes
We walk the grassy ramparts till they break
In a steep gradient to the ancient gate.
I take your arm for comfort and support
On the rough, downward, outward slope.
Content, in age, that passion's melted into
The amiable symbiosis of long marriage.

HISTORY IS NOW

When I was a child the world stood still:
People and prices were unchanged,
Trains were many and cars were few,
Life seemed settled and well-arranged.

This was not always so, I knew,
I learned in History of the Past,
But Now, where I lived, seemed fixed and I
Thought that this state would always last.

Mines were mined and steel was worked
Shipyards were busy and ships and crew
Travelled the seas; and families
Were the only nuclear things we knew.

But now –
Coal mines and slate quarries are museums;
The infernal glow has faded from the sky
Above the steelworks; and grass grows
Upon the slipways in the yards. Few ships
Now sail with merchandise; the docks
Spawn houses for the rich and pleasure gardens.

So what is left to do to make a living?
Only to take in one another's cooking –
History has caught up with me –

History is Now.

DRAWING THE LINE

On the last day of the old year we drove
Past the calm, resting winter woods and fields
Towards the sea. Walking then through the dunes,
We heard the waves roar over a strand that yields
To the tide's onslaught. Twice a day for ever
The sea conquers the land and then retreats,
And season follows season through the year,
Plants bud and flower and fruit, nature repeats
Inexorably her steady gradual change.
The seeds are formed before the flowers fall
New plans are laid before the old's fulfilled,
An orderly succession governs all.

Only we humans, time-obsessed, insist
On sharp distinctions, drawing a neat line
Between the end of one phase and the next:
Today is eighty-eight, tomorrow eighty-nine.

RHINE JOURNEY

We cruised in comfort slowly down the Rhine
Poplars, acacias, willows shading green,
Warm sunshine over all; the clambering vines
The Romans brought still overlook the scene.

Romans, barbarians, medieval knights,
Archbishop - princes, emperors – all here led
Marching and counter-march, laid bare the land
Of common people, starved, diseased and dead.

So many centuries of violence –
Wars of religion, who should rule which land,
Castles, cathedrals and whole cities too
Destroyed, rebuilt, destroyed again, re-planned.

But now, the river flows through lands at peace;
After some forty years the countries here
Can meet in council, can forswear the past,
Join in attempts to live removed from fear.

> In Freiburg all the bells were rung,
> In the wide square the mass was sung;
> Past shuttered shops, through empty street
> The Old Town echoed to our feet
> That Holy day.

> In Strasbourg, storks, nesting and flying,
> Bring back new life where once was dying.
> The clockwork people marking Time's
> Passage from warring in their chimes,
> To a new way.

And Mainz, where Gutenburg had been,
Where the first printed books were seen.
'In the beginning was the Word'
Mightier, more lasting than the sword –
Or so we say.

High on the Dragon-Mountain top
The labouring train comes to a stop
And far down river, where Bonn lies,
East and West talk and make new ties
We pray will stay.

In Coventry the people pray:
'Father forgive'. We too must say
Forgive us all – may we forgive
Old hurts, injustices – and live
In peace today.

But home at last, we hardly enter
Till loud bombs shatter the town centre.
Through myth and mists the fighting lives
No one forgets and none forgives
And we all pay.

When shall we reach a time when we can match
Flags of old enemies together streaming?
When can we sit (like Micah in his dreaming)
Under our vines, in our potato patch?

THIS TIME

Autumn has always seemed the time of hope and new
beginnings.
For Spring, though full of promise,
Slips into Summer unfulfilled.
But when that first chill is felt
Behind the last lazy, hazy sunshine,
When hedgerows are hung
With the false early frost of old man's beard
And scarlet and crimson of rosehip and haw,
Then comes the time for us to say:
'This Time'.

This time, all will be different and better.
At school, there was a new class and new, unsullied
books.
This time there would be no blots, no corrections,
And the most irregular of verbs would flow smoothly
Over the clean page.
Much later,
When the children returned to school
After long, active summer days,
This time I would read all the books,
Sew on all the buttons,
Tidy all the drawers,
Carry out all the plans.
And though I now knew all this to be unlikely,

Still I thought, as I walked in the cooling sunshine and
the painted leaves,
'This time –'

But this time, in the end, proves finite.
Time is spent, lost or wasted.
The hint of frost on an autumn morning gives warning
That mortality, in little waves,
Laps like the tide about our feet.

Some time, this time will be the last time.
Some time, there will be time no more.

TRANSIT CAMP

The limes that line the avenue were bare
When first we came; out in the car park
Two chestnuts hung grey branches like long hair
Blowing untidily in early dark.
The flat was small and cold and damp, and I,
Arriving breathless up the echoing stair,
Saw the far hills and open evening sky
Over the neighbours' garden walls, and where
A church spire pointed through a tossing bough.

We watched the buds swell and the small green leaves
Grow till they blotted church and hills. And now
The candles burn and fall; summer achieves
Full foliage and warmth and glowing sun.

At length a rusty look on chestnut shows,
The conkers fall, the cycle's nearly done;
The limes are faintly jaundiced, cool wind blows,
Autumn is come, the trees grow bare, and so
Now that the leaves are gone, may we not go?

'THE NAGGING SEED'

Poems lead lives of great irregularity:
From conception to delivery is quite
Unpredictable. Times of gestation
Vary enormously; one can lose sight
As it were, that anything is forming.
Sometimes ideas and phrases seem to grow
So very fast and so felicitously
That the whole piece is finished and on show
Within a day or two. But then, sometimes,
Weeks, months and even many years go by
And only half-forgotten sentences
May nudge us to remind us where they lie.
Perhaps a poem can lie dormant like
The second egg of the Red Kangaroo,
Growing when circumstances are auspicious?
And some, perhaps, will never come in view
But die, be reabsorbed and reappear,
Words and ideas recycled, formed anew.

But when the poem stirs and grows apace
And nears full term and can be born at last
Our labour is complete, the verses live,
The long, the nagging waiting time is past.
'Safely delivered' – notice pinned, news filed –
No royal baby, but my own dear child.

IN THE MUSEUM

A previous collection of verse took its title from the first poem; the title of this collection comes from the last one. It is certainly true that with age the past becomes more familiar and the present more alien; the future of course is personally largely irrelevant. Even the structure of most of my verse is old-fashioned and is, like me, quite comfortable in the muscum.

Joyce Neill
March 1997

2. IN THE MUSEUM

HALCYON DAYS   (Cease-fire: 13.10.94)

Our halcyon days came earlier than in legend.
And in this recent still, calm, shining spell
The new-hatched chicks of peace float on a sea
Becalmed, after its troubled storm-waves fell.
Mist mars our vision still; but soon the light
Grows after solstice and bright birds take flight.

DARK AGES

Some sixteen hundred years ago or more
The Roman Britons talked on a winter's night
In their warm villas, while they still had slaves
To service hypocausts well out of sight.
'The news from Gaul's not good: barbarians
Are infiltrating there'. Another said:
'They say a further legion left last week;
The eagles are departing; who will head
Defence of home and city when they go?
Our Pax and Lex Romana grow more weak,
The life our fathers led disintegrates,
The lights are dimmed, the future grows more bleak'.

Now we, in turn, talk in our heated rooms,
(Warmer than any since those Roman times).
We like them, worried: our barbarians
Are through the gates and in our midst; the signs
Are there for all to see. We lock our doors
Against the mugger, terrorist and thief.
Our Lex and Pax are now a thin veneer
Beneath which chaos lurks; the time is brief.
Civilizations rise and fall, and so
Darkness may come again for us, full cycle,
Sooner rather than later; so we should
Keep the boat ready for Skellig Michael.

NEW BABEL

Now Babel's tower is built for us again,
New words and phrases must be newly born.
We used to talk: increasingly it seems
Dialogue skills are what we need to spawn.
'How are you getting on?' we used to say,
'And are you needing any changes made?'
Performance Indicators now can tell
When to Interpolate Adjustment Aid.
'We're a bit short of this or that,' we'd say;
Now our Resources Allocations fail;
Consumer-led Demand, new Targeting
Ensure that at all this we do not quail.
We must consult our colleagues and indulge
In Interface Communication,
And we must bow to Market-Driven Forces
If we would keep our place in this new nation.

Oh! I must learn to Diarise my life
And Minimise old phrases now left waiting,
Reform my language, Jargonise my words
And Maximise my Professional Updating.

THE BARBARY APE AT NAVAN FORT

Across the miles, across the years,
Sharing wry smiles, mingling our tears
The little Barbary ape and I
Greet one another with a sigh.
Alas, poor ape, your tiny skull
Reproaches me from the glass wall
Of your new home: a twilit tomb
Within this dim, sepulchral room.
I think about you shivering here
In this cool land; your scanty fur
Inadequate against the breeze
Tossing the falling autumn leaves,
Or the soft Irish rains which fall
Inexorably over all.
And did you dream of warmer lands,
Of palm trees waving feathered hands?
Of other chattering apes that share
The sunshine and the blue skies there?
We both were strangers here – but I
Came willingly, with open eye
And those I love; but little you
Came frightened, cold and lonely too.
Oh Barbary ape – for you I weep -
Dead long ago and buried deep.

PORTRAITS OF DESPAIR

1.
Most faces on the Obituary page
Are of the old; they die full of achievement
And of years.
So the first shock is to see this younger face
Look back at us; he has died too soon
Inviting our tears.

He spent his life on Green and peaceful causes
So when his caring
Turned to despairing
He climbed up a tree, an apricot tree,
And there among the small gold glowing globes,
He hanged himself, you see.

2.
There is no picture of this one alive.
In crowds of refugees, she died quite alone,
Not even her name was known.
But we see her, her back turned to us
And her face hidden in the trunk of the tree.
Do you know what it looked like at first to me?
Like someone playing Grandmother's Footsteps
Who would turn suddenly on the advancing hordes
And shout: 'Back, all of you, and heed my words!'

But then I read that when all her hope
Was gone, she made for herself a rope
Out of her belt and twisted scarf – and hanged herself.
I see now that her feet don't touch the ground
And she can never, ever again, turn round.

SEARCHING

Some of us thought we heard the whales
But none of us saw them.
We saw seals bobbing, and we saw shearwaters
Wheeling and skimming;
And we saw dolphins – oh, the dolphins!
Leaping and playing,
With such joy and friendship, such abandon!
Our hearts leapt with them.
But even when the boatman stopped the engines
And silence enfolded us,
The fog swirled still more closely round us there;
And that was when
Some of us thought we heard the whales
But none of us saw them.

CONFORMITY – Or Megan at four months.

Megan *fach* lies in her dear mother's lap
And counts her fingers.
The answer is seldom the same twice
And a doubt lingers
That, like waving anemones as the tide rises,
The number can vary,
So she concentrates hard and counts them again,
For that thought makes her wary.

But soon, like the rest of us, she will conform
In her counting – and then
The tedious fact will emerge every time
That the answer is ten.

IN HOSPITAL

In four short days, within four sterile walls,
I glide through decades back to nursery ways:
Lie down to sleep and waken when I'm bid,
Relinquishing the ordering of my days.

This I, who for so many years has lived
Obsessionally organising Time,
Drops into Limbo, levitating there,
No problems posed except to find a rhyme.

And, by the kindness of the Ladies' Guild,
A mini-set reports the distant scene
Of puny wars, tiny catastrophes,
Cut down to fit my shrunken, personal screen.

ISMENE

What happened to Ismene? I don't know,
Does anyone? The play is silent.
It is Antigone who dominates
The scene, and she whom none can make relent.
Antigone, made of fine-tempered steel,
Unyielding in her certainty of choice,
Sure that the laws of gods take precedence
Over the sound of tyrant's human voice.
And she is right; I am quite sure of that.

But when the sisters met that second time,
And when Ismene begged to die with her
In the closed cell, do we detect a sign
That sacrifice and glory are not shared
With others made of common, yielding clay,
Whose natures still bar the heroic gesture?
Each can be loving only in her way,
Ewe lambs and lionesses don't lie down
Together. So – what was Ismene's fate?
Did she live on and marry and have children,
To live their lives through tragedy and hate?
Or did she take that same, sad, swift short-cut
Taken to Hades by her aunt and mother
And sister? There to be joined at last
With all her tragic line, parents and brother,
So that the family finally could rest?
That would be brave too; that would be best.

GOLDEN MYCENAE

Golden Mycenae, rising from the plain,
Could still send haunted shivers down the back,
As, through the Lion gate, we followed those
Whose chariots made the deeply-worn stone track.
High in the ruined citadel I found,
Amongst the stones, white cyclamen that grow,
And saw, just where the reflexed petals turned
From the flower's heart, a deep red colour flow.
Blood of avenger and avenged spilled so
From Atreus' House millennia ago.

REFLECTIONS

Mirror, mirror on the wall
Do you tell the truth at all?
The image that looks back at me
Is that what other people see?

Sometimes the physical eye can modify
And change the image;
Etiolated Modigliani
Figures are what he saw,
The muted colours of an aging painter
Betray the blurred lens.
But the mind's eye, the imagined picture
Are from another stage,
Another drama is unfolding there,
And takes the floor.
The individual imagination
Can modify men's
Perceptions; and it is perception
That is unique.
Perception: formed from imagination
And from our milieu,
Picasso people, seen by the inward eye
Linked with the soul,
Prophetic understanding, making some
New words to speak.
Then, too, a partial blindness, forcing some
To turn, to revere
False gods that lead astray, and to lose sight
Of the true goal.

Mirror, mirror on the wall,
You hardly tell the truth at all;
The images that there I see
Belong peculiarly to me.

HOMAGE TO THE PRESIDENT

(To Mary Robinson, President of Ireland)

We come to pay our homage
To one who breaks the mould
Of woman's place in Ireland
Accepted from of old.
A place once largely hidden
From seats of power and law,
An influence vicarious
Was most that went before.

Not Deirdre of the Sorrows
Nor Maeve, the Warrior Queen.
Nor yet storm-tossed Fionnuala
Sheltering the boys between
Her outstretched, feathered arms;
Nor grief-torn Juno praying –
(Though all of these are with us.)
For now we can be saying -

That you have shown us clearly
That women, too, with men
Can carry weighty matters
And bring fresh views to them.
And warm, concerned, approachable,
Wife, mother, stateswoman too,
You listen to all people
And hear our points of view.

For under the same changing sky
And blown by common winds,
Subject to the same griefs and joys
We have our varying minds.
We need each other always,
Men, women, Planter and Gael,
So – Homage to the President!
We greet you now – All Hail!

NOT ONLY IN THE BELFRY

(An Irish zoologist has observed that some species of
bats in Ireland always prefer to nest in a church of
their chosen denomination).

The Irish bats are cultured creatures:
Among their interesting features
Is the ability to choose
To nest according to their views.
The Long-Eared bats have Roman leanings,
Natterers seek Anglican ceilings,
And church or chapel still divides
Chiroptologicalist sides.
Must even bats in Ireland thus
Maintain sectarian strife and fuss?
But Pipistrelles can give us hope,
At home with or without the Pope;
And, being also very small,
Perhaps may nest in Gospel Hall?
Might even haunt a Quaker Meeting,
Their high-pitched squeak giving a fleeting
Message of Reconcilation
To the divided Irish nation.

TEMPUS FUGIT

I watched you walking down the drive,
White-haired, with a slight stoop,
And saw you fifty years ago,
One of a waiting group
Collected in the platform's gloom
Of wartime's blacked-out night,
To meet the weary passengers
Beginning to alight.
And my tall love I could not miss -
You only stooped then for our kiss.

FOR VIRGINIA

The day you went, the autumn came
With cool dawn mist and heavy dew
And glistening spiders' webs to frame
The doorway where we waved to you.
Summer was only here in name
While you were with us, it is true,
But spite of cloud and wind and rain
Our summer and our sun were you.
 So, when you went, the autumn came
With mists and spiders' webs and dew.

FOR MEG

You gave me a golden day:
From early, empty English lanes,
Across the sea
To sunlit roads of Picardy;
A day stolen from time.

Under the lime trees' shade,
Beside the once blood-stained river,
Sipping my *thé citron,*
The peaceful Sunday family parade
Flows past us.
I hear again the French voices
(And those clever, fluent toddlers!)
Boats sail dreamlike to and fro
As the river mingles with the sea.
All this you gave to me.

When every other day
Has gone its way
Your golden timeless day
Will stay.

RACHEL'S DONEGAL

In the dream world of Rachel's Donegal
The hills withdraw into a haze of heat:
The western sea is deep Aegean blue:
Its warm waves lap our feet.

Dear Rachel, how do you make it come to pass?
You can control the weather – us as well;
The seagulls call you (on their mobile phones?)
We are all under your spell!

K156

Once, at my breakfast, unexpected tears
Sprang to my eyes; music from long ago
Had wrenched me back to hear a small boy say:
'Can you, too, hear another tune below
The top one? I can, and it goes like this:-'
He hummed it perfectly. Why was I made,
Remembering that moment from the past,
To weep so bitterly on marmalade?

FOR LEX, ON HER EIGHTEENTH BIRTHDAY, 7/7/92.

No longer little Lecky Becky
(not always early now for brekky)
At eighteen you are now grown-up
With your opinions all sewn up
You had a latch-key long ago,
But now you have the vote – and so –
I hope you'll give a passing thought
To your great-grandmother who fought
With others taking part in demos,
Carrying banners, writing memos,
So that a later generation
Could make its mark within the nation.
Should you opt out, or worse, forget
You owe them all a weighty debt,
You'll hear a whirring underground:
Pankhurst et al will not sleep sound.

Now dearest Lex, may happy days
And Fortune smile on you always.

WHY ME?

I think Job asked the wrong question:
Not why? – why not?
Death and disaster and disease
Are our human lot:
And if we seem to escape
And get off scot-
Free – still the question remains
Not why – why not?

But when affliction does strike down,
What then we need
Is not a court of divine law
In which to plead,
But certainty of God-with-us.
His Light, His Seed,
His Comforter are here
To meet our need.

IN THE BEGINNING -

It wasn't like that.
I think that, by the time they wrote it down,
It had to explain what they were experiencing then.
And, of course, by then he did take precedence,
And, of course, he was the boss.
And if she owed her existence to just one rib
She would be pretty inferior.
(Though the Church Fathers went further:
Woman was a defective man.
As soon say man is an aberrant woman,
Running destructively to muscle and power and
violence.)

They must surely have hoped that life was once
paradisal;
It couldn't always have been short and brutish.
So whose fault was it?
'Not mine!' he said
'Not mine!' she said (though he thought it was!)
So they blamed the serpent:
An early case of transference
Or of a childish alter ego who is our shadow persona.

And then, all that hierarchy:
Dominion over the plants and animals,
And naming them – the ultimate in ownership;
No question of discussion or cooperation.
'Be fruitful and multiply' – well the world was empty
then, but not now.
And the punishment after the disobedience;
Bringing forth children; pain and effort and hard work,
certainly
But did they not realise? In the end, not Sorrow – Joy!

In the beginning, the very beginning,
God created The Heavens and the Earth
He said: 'Let there be…' and there was;
'Male and female created he them…'simultaneously.
And the power of the Spirit was, and still is, over all.

ABSENT GODS

In the great shadow of the absent gods
We grope for truth and certainty and meaning.
But Harvest's done; for us, only the gleaning
Of what remains after the reaper plods
Homewards. The centuries of common learning,
Accepted rules, measuring how we live,
Shared values, and assurances that give
Hopes of a heaven to satisfy our yearning –

All these are gathered in, into that shade.
We now drift rudderless on uncharted seas,
And worship Mammon; the old myths destroyed,
Forgotten in a chaos we have made.
But still, we painful pilgrims on our knees,
Seek for new light to penetrate this void.

ANCHORAGE

My sailing friend gave me this lovely image
Of boats, moored to a common cable,
The cable anchored firm and deep below.
On the calm water of the anchorage
The boats float still and steady, but yet able
Gently to swing when the small breezes blow.

He thinks of this in Meeting as Friends sit,
Separate to the superficial gaze,
Though unseen links will join us deep below.
Our sight turns in and finds the pathway lit
So we can turn from our disparate ways
And feel the Spirit, like small breezes, blow.

PSALM 19 (Paraphrase)

In the still beauty of the evening sky
Before the mysterious dusk's retiring glow,
In the immaculate promise of the dawn
The Spirit moves, I know.

As from the sun's apparent daily journey
The earth receives its light and heat and power,
So Holy Spirit moves through all creation
Empowering every hour.

In the continuing drama of the earth
We have our steps to dance, our words to say.
We must keep to our script, our choreography,
We must not stray.

PSALM 22

Where had it gone, the once unquestioning faith
Of childhood ways?
How can I carry the continuing doubts
That haunt my days?
Life's lack of meaning and my worthlessness
Both obsess me;
I gaze with paranoia at the world
Which mocks to see
How sickness and infirmity can replace
My once sure health,
My certainty of hope and of salvation,
My infinite wealth.

I must turn round with due humility,
Posit again
Power of the Spirit to strengthen and support
And ease the pain,
And so in time perhaps, I may yet learn
Experientially, faith can return.

ENTERING IN

What is it like, to be another person?
How does it feel, starting from a strange place?
How would we think, growing within a milieu
That sees the same world with a different face?

We start with gender: how does the other feel?
A child with parents: wanted – or the reverse:
Raised in security to self-esteem
Or born to see our future hopes disperse.

If we were poor, watching our children die,
How would we see (though dimly through our tears)
The rich, whose children, sheltered, warmed and fed,
Can grow and prosper through their lengthening years?

So many opposites drawing dividing lines:
Catholic and Protestant, Arab and Jew;
Soldier and Pacifist, Women and Men,
Christian and Muslim, Muslim and Hindu –
Needs must accept and recognise all truths
And their validity, equal in worth
And in significance; experienced by
And coloured in each one of us from birth.

'Except ye be converted' and can change
And shed the assumed accretions of the years
Muffling us since our childhood's open vision,
And nourishing our prejudice and fears,
'Ye shall in no wise enter in' – not only
Experiences from other human parts,
But barred, he said, from entering the Kingdom
Or from receiving it within our hearts.

THAT OF GOD

One snowy morning, having time to kill,
He turned aside to contemplate the dead
Within their cemetery. He felt a hand
Pluck at his sleeve and turned to see a nun
Advanced in years, who begged his arm's support.
In my mind's eye I see them clearly there:
The two dark figures sharp against the snow,
Watched by the looming lines of headstones, crosses,
And funeral urns.
They progress slowly on the slippery path,
She leaning on his arm, he bending low
To catch her words.
Returning to the gates, they said goodbye.
'I hoped for help', she said, 'I think God sent you'.
Well – did he?
There was no overt message,
No words heard; only a chance decision
Of the moment, to turn towards the graves.
But did she see that through him God would help?
Proofs have no place and we can make no tests
Within the realm of hope and faith and love.

THE MALEVOLENCE OF INANIMATE OBJECTS

I have observed that as I grow older
Inanimate objects grow bolder and bolder:
Cups leap from my hands and crash to the ground,
The papers I need, hide, and cannot be found.
Pills jump from their bottles, roll under the table,
And I, being stiff, am no longer able
To crouch down and retrieve them; and, sadly, I fear,
That I will not see them – my specs are not here.
I have long been convinced that my glasses can walk
But when asked where they are they're unable to talk.
My car keys, I think, are part of these plots,
And my shoe laces end up as Gordian Knots.
So what can be done all these things to placate?
Could a truce be arranged? Or is it too late?

CONGESTION

I think of my brain
As a tightly packed train
On the London Underground,
Where nobody can
Get out or get in
And no way to the door can be found.
And new information
Gets left at the station,
While facts lost to sight
All fail to alight.
Oh! What can I do to remove this great block?
I need (but won't get) some new rolling stock.

THREE IN THE MORNING

Sometimes, around three in the morning
And quite without warning,
My lovely healing sleep
Slips clean away.
Then from the darkest corners creep
The ugly thoughts that through the day
I keep at bay.
So now I feel again
Old anger, and old pain,
And old regrets for things done and left undone.
And when I turn to see
What yet may be,
I fear for what's to come.
How long will wits and functions take to leave,
As death plucks at my sleeve,
Until he finally gains full attention?
When, without further intervention,
I hope I may
Like sleep, slip clean away.

ONCE UPON A TIME

Once upon a time
When skies (but never you)
Were always blue,
When every word
Spoken, was heard:
There, like a song no longer sung,
Is the tune called: 'When-the-children-were-young'.

It is a parcel, neatly stored,
Beneath a floorboard
Of the mind.
You may not find
All was as you had imagined;

So it is best
To let it rest.

IN THE MUSEUM

I am in the Museum – the top floor,
Among the paintings and the toys:
Pictures and emblems of past scenes and pastimes.
The Giant's Causeway, born of legend,
Cut down to size by Johnson:
('Worth seeing but not worth going to see'.)
Quiet Victorian watercolours, where cattle graze and
now houses jostle:
Familiar landscapes and known local faces.

From their glass houses, dolls return glassy stares and
fixed smiles.
Some child loved them once, as I did mine.
One is a baby doll, a replica of mine whom I called
Mair,
(I was in my Welsh period then.)

On through the paintings, past the startled and startling
nuns,
Till from the window I look out
Over the sprawling, damaged city struggling to right
itself – but how? And when?
Far out beyond rises Cave Hill, old fort and haunt of
briefly united Irishmen,
Divided and defensive still.

My Irish period has gone on too long;
Time now to sink into these padded seats
And on this quiet weekday morning remember
I am in the Museum.

LAST POEMS

These poems, which remained uncollected until now, were written since the other two collections appeared in print. Aided by a word-processor I managed to 'get them down'. They record, in a sense, more of the same: some light-hearted and hopeful, some sombrely aware of Time's action on our lives.

Joyce Neill
February 2007

3. LAST POEMS

CHRISTMAS 1998

Last Christmas wasn't very jolly:
Not a single sprig of holly
Or of mistletoe;
No pendant stocking did I see
Nor any trace of christmas tree
And not one flake of snow.
But a robin left his christmas card
To sing a greeting in our yard.

OPERATION

All day we waited; in the afternoon
You then withdrew
To that strange limbo lost to memory.
I waited without you
And heard with thankfulness the news was good,
But waited still
Until the evening in the dim-lit ward;
I gazed my fill
As you slipped gently in and out of sleep,
With a faint smile.

Then I recalled a sketch made years ago
And saw the while
Dark curls, gold lighted; eyes closed on round cheeks
As yours were there,
I saw again the child that once you were,
So small and dear.

You stirred, opened your eyes and smiled at me,
And I could see
My lovely, dark-eyed, reborn daughter here
Restored to me.

DIAMOND WEDDING

Old man, old man, I sit and I look:
I know your name – it is still the same -
But what about you?
Retreating to newspapers, or a book,
What now, I wonder, can remain
Of that young man that once I knew,
That He who literally could sweep
Me from my feet? Whom now I weep.

Old woman, old woman – a fine one to talk!
Wrinkled and slow and crabby I know,
So what about you?
Daily you take your boring walk;
The nubile girl I left long ago,
When her joints grew stiff and her grey hairs grew
And the world grew strange and the paths grew steep.
Sixty years should suffice: for you both I weep.

IS THERE A POINT?

Here I sit, waiting to die,
Hard of hearing and blind in one eye,
Aching and stiff in muscle and joint
And I ask myself: 'Well, what is the POINT?'
Closely followed by question two:
'Does there have to BE any point for you?'
Does there have to be a Master Plan
A clerk of works or a Superman?
If we want to find a way through the wood
Is it not sufficient to try to be good?
With help, of course, from example and word
Of preachers and teachers whose voices are heard,
Echoing down the changing years,
Where words change too, but not our fears.

ON A MAY MORNING

Down by the river bank, on a May morning
Beauty enfolded me:
Bluebells and stitchwort and tall Queen Anne's lace,
New buttercups to see;
The generous fresh green grass beneath my feet,
Birdsong from every tree.

All the May mornings of a lifetime's springs
Were there for me distilled
And I was drunk upon this distillate
With which I then was filled.
The sunlight dazzled and the bright sky sang
While the green world was stilled.

And of the unattended moment there
I, too, was then a part,
For the creative spirit all-pervading
Was also in my heart;
So no one there could say where this 'I' ends
Or where the rest may start.

THE COFFIN SHIP

If I am part of the glory
Then the horror must also be mine;
So the coffin ship in Mayo
At the foot of Patrick's climb
Lays heavily on my shoulders
Its weight of sorrow and pain;
And guilt for the death and suffering
Shown starkly here again.

A ship in a field must startle
With raggedy sails and mast;
When now you approach more closely
You will gaze on this ship aghast.
For the sails you find are skeletons,
A cross crowns the top of each mast:
The Coffin Ship is filled with the dead
Of all famines and wrongs in the past.

So if I am part of the glory
The horrors must also be mine:
The oceans of Light and of Darkness
Remain till the end of time.

JUBILATE

On twenty-eight O-seven O-one
Our one and only darling son
Completes his first half-century
(And this, of course, will mean for me
That I've no child now under fifty
So with my time I must be thrifty.
I think I'll wear white lacy caps,
And also take more frequent naps;
A shawl may now appear de rigeur
To hide my more unshapely figure.)

But what I really want to say
To you on this auspicious day
Is that we send much love to you
And to dear Lynn in all you do
Together through all future times
And birthdays not yet formed in rhymes.
So may you have, in Gay Paree,
A really splendid JUBILEE!

HIBERNATION

I do admire the grizzly bear,
The dormouse and the tortoise,
For they know how to hibernate,
Avoiding winter - which I hate -
And all the ills it's brought us.

We'd sleep through all the ice and snow,
Cold wind and rain until
We'd wake refreshed and slim, and rise,
Changed from eighteen to twelve in size,
To greet a bright, warm April.

So all you physiologists
Stop thinking about Space;
Turn your research to hibernation,
Suggest some needed alteration
To save the human race.

For thus we'd use less oil and gas,
Read fewer books and papers;
The trees would grow unchecked, and holes
In ozone layers would fail feared goals
Through loss of evil vapours.

HARVEST HYMN FOR CHRISTIAN AID

City dwellers such as we,
Far removed from field and plough,
What know we of Harvest Home?
How can thanks be given now?

Other parts of our one world
Still know drought, their harvests fail,
Famine haunts our neighbours there
Still we hear their children wail.

We have food enough to share
To feed the hungry in their need:
Our brethren, of whom Jesus said
We give to Him when these we feed.

Let us therefore in one world,
Whether feast or famine reign,
Feed all God's family, and share
His gift of love that eases pain.

PLANTING PEAS (or Ps)

Two plump pigeons perch in the trees,
Waiting for me to plant my peas.
Then they plan to swoop down when I am away,
Peck the peas from the ground and call it a day.
But I can plan too and I plan to defeat'em
With pea-sticks to climb, and netting to beat'em.
In the fullness of time it is I that will eat'em
(The peas not the pigeons tho' they've plenty of meat on.)

FRÄULEIN BUXTEHUDE

Alas for Fräulein Buxtehude,
It seems that no one ever wooed her.
She might have been Frau J S Bach
Or Mrs G F Handel,
Even, perhaps, Frau Matheson …
But yet no breath of scandal
Or passion ever touched her name
Which therefore still remained the same.
Even when Papa's post was proffered
And Fräulein B was 'special offered'
The applicants as one withdrew
(She must have been a proper shrew!)
Alas! Poor Fräulein Buxtehude,
No charms had she, so no one wooed her.

FOR KATHLEEN CUTHBERT, after a *most*
enjoyable luncheon party, May 10th 2002

A major pleasure, at this stage
Of our increasingly great age,
Is sitting down to take our ease
With lively, bright contempories;
And, to augment our happy mood,
Provision of delicious food.

Then from this common vantage point,
The strange new world's less out of joint,
And the old shared one's warm and clear,
Amid the snows of yesteryear.
So, Kathleen, here to you I send
My grateful thanks for a dear friend.

AFTER THE JOURNEY

After the journey, what then shall we find
On our return? Things will not be the same.
That square space where we fitted easily
May house another, with an unknown name.
In any case it may today be found
We are no longer square, we are turned round.

And that being so, where do we now belong?
After the sights we've seen, the deeds we've done
How could we not be changed? Who are we now?
From our experiences, new roles are won;
And we ourselves are altered, taking a road
Different from the old path that once we strode.

GOING HOME

When my mother was dying, 'I want
To go home,' she said.
But I thought: 'You are home here with us,
We are all at your bed.'
For I thought she was talking of Wales, where
She was born and reared,
And where no one remained from that time now,
No known voice would be heard.

But I know now that home is our childhood,
Is in time, not space:
For its safety and comfort and order
Can be any place.
Now I, too, would like to go back there …
- Not to my old town –
Then as a good child at the meal's end say:
'Please may I get down?'

NUNC DIMITTIS

The day begins: Time, measured in hours,
Loiters towards the night.
But, measured in years, it races to an end
Not clearly yet in sight.
Those years were full and busy, but the hours
Are empty now.
I have had good measure and good company
In the past show.
And as I move along
To an end drawing near,
In the distance I hear
The sound of Simeon's Song.

SONNET – ON HER BLINDNESS
July 2002

In the crepuscular world where I now live
All trees are olive trees: pale, silvery green.
People I meet have Francis Bacon faces
Newly acquired since previously seen.
All steps and stairs are unreliable now,
Their edges undulate as I advance:
To try to climb without a banister
Is to attempt a risky game of chance.
I cannot read instructions on a packet,
Nor set machines to do as I require:
Kind voices read to me, as once in childhood,
From so-called 'books' which can be had on hire.
As the scene shrinks, the lengthy hours expand,
Time drags me, slow and groping, by the hand.

A SOMBRE SONNET

When I consider how my Time is spent;
Hours that have loitered, and the years that race,
And islands that Time seemed to circumvent,
Or it stood still in a remembered place…
Then Time, it seems, has its own Stock Exchange,
Can vary both in value and in size;
Childhoods seem endless, in their narrow range,
While most Time else proverbially flies.
Decades can disappear now overnight,
Easter recurs with last year's eggs scarce found;
My Time, it seems, is running out of sight,
I, here in limbo, listen to the sound
Of ticking slowing down. Soon now the door
Will close upon the clock: there will be Time no more.

INDEX

Printed in the United Kingdom
by Lightning Source UK Ltd.
121309UK00001B/187-234/A

9 780755 210640